Hazelwood v. *Kuhlmeier* and the School Newspaper Censorship Debate

Debating Supreme Court Decisions

Titles in the *Debating Supreme Court Decisions* Series

The *Bakke* Case and the Affirmative Action Debate
Debating Supreme Court Decisions
ISBN 0-7660-2526-8

***Clay* v. *United States* and How Muhammad Ali Fought the Draft**
Debating Supreme Court Decisions
ISBN 0-7660-2393-1

***Cruzan* v. *Missouri* and the Right to Die Debate**
Debating Supreme Court Decisions
ISBN 0-7660-2356-7

The *Earls* Case and the Student Drug Testing Debate
Debating Supreme Court Decisions
ISBN 0-7660-2478-4

***Furman* v. *Georgia* and the Death Penalty Debate**
Debating Supreme Court Decisions
ISBN 0-7660-2390-7

The *Gault* Case and Young People's Rights
Debating Supreme Court Decisions
ISBN 0-7660-2476-8

***Hazelwood* v. *Kuhlmeier* and the School Newspaper Censorship Debate**
Debating Supreme Court Decisions
ISBN 0-7660-2394-X

***Lemon* v. *Kurtzman* and the Separation of Church and State Debate**
Debating Supreme Court Decisions
ISBN 0-7660-2391-5

***Miranda* v. *Arizona* and the Rights of the Accused**
Debating Supreme Court Decisions
ISBN 0-7660-2477-6

***New York Times* v. *Sullivan* and the Freedom of the Press Debate**
Debating Supreme Court Decisions
ISBN 0-7660-2357-5

***Schenck* v. *United States* and the Freedom of Speech Debate**
Debating Supreme Court Decisions
ISBN 0-7660-2392-3

***Tinker* v. *Des Moines* and Students' Right to Free Speech**
Debating Supreme Court Decisions
ISBN 0-7660-2538-1

Hazelwood v. Kuhlmeier and the School Newspaper Censorship Debate

Debating Supreme Court Decisions

Tracy A. Phillips

Enslow Publishers, Inc.
40 Industrial Road
Box 398
Berkeley Heights, NJ 07922
USA

http://www.enslow.com

Library of Congress Cataloging-in-Publication Data

Phillips, Tracy A.
    Hazelwood v. Kuhlmeier and the school newspaper censorship debate : debating
    Supreme Court decisions / Tracy A. Phillips.
        p. cm. — (Debating Supreme Court decisions)
    Includes bibliographical references and index.
    ISBN 0-7660-2394-X
    1. Hazelwood School District—Trials, litigation, etc. 2. Kuhlmeier, Cathy—Trials,
        litigation, etc. 3. Student newspapers and periodicals—Censorship—Missouri.
        I. Title. II. Title: Hazelwood versus Kuhlmeier. III. Series.
    KF228.H397P48 2006
    342.7308'53—dc22

                                    2005034655

Printed in the United States of America

10 9 8 7 6 5 4 3 2 1

To Our Readers: We have done our best to make sure that all Internet Addresses in this
book were active and appropriate when we went to press. However, the author and
publisher have no control over and assume no liability for the material available on those
Internet sites or on other Web sites they may link to. Any comments or suggestions can be
sent by e-mail to comments@enslow.com or to the address on the back cover.

Illustration Credits: AP/Wide World, p. 93; Electronic Design of Ithaca and the Student
Press Law Center, p. 85; copyright 1988 Engelhardt in the *St. Louis Post-Dispatch*,
reprinted with permission, p. 77; Harris & Ewing, collection of the Supreme Court of the
United States, p. 66; Hazelwood East High School *Spectrum*, May 13, 1983, unpublished
articles, pp. 48–49; Hazelwood School District Yearbook, p. 40; Hemera Image Express,
p. 4; Library of Congress, p. 59; photo by Drake Mabry, copyright 1965, the Des Moines
Register and Tribune Company, reprinted with permission, p. 73; St. Louis Post-Dispatch,
pp. 31; copyright 1990 Bob Sacha, p. 22; St. Louis Globe-Democrat Archives of the
St. Louis Mercantile Library at the University of Missouri-St. Louis, p. 10.

Cover Illustrations: Background, Artville; photograph, St. Louis Post-Dispatch.

Contents

chapter 1

Censorship 101

The words *divorce, abortion,* and *pregnancy* filled articles written by Hazelwood East High School students for their upcoming May 13, 1983 edition of *Spectrum,* the school-sponsored newspaper. A last-minute decision to censor various elements of the May 13 edition of *Spectrum* by school officials would lead to a legal debate that would make its way to the United States Supreme Court. At the heart of the debate would be the freedom of expression, the right to free speech, and the freedom of the press. School officials had decided to censor certain articles in the edition because one article featured pregnant students of Hazelwood East and another discussed students who had divorced parents. The student staff of the newspaper was not consulted before the censorship occurred. What ensued was a very lengthy and public legal battle that would determine the rights of students with regard to freedom of expression in public schools. The lawsuit would span years and take these students on a journey through the American justice system, the likes of which could not be taught in any civics class in the country.

Hazelwood East High School is a relatively large high school in Hazelwood, Missouri, a suburb of St. Louis. Like many large high schools, Hazelwood East has an array of student activities available to the student body. Some students participate in sports and clubs; others work as staff on the school newspaper. To be a staff member of *Spectrum,* a student had to be enrolled in the Journalism II class. Students who were not enrolled in the class could, however, submit articles for publication even though they were not permitted to be staff members of *Spectrum.* Working on the newspaper was the primary activity of the Journalism II class. Once students completed Journalism I, a class that taught the basics of how to publish a newspaper, they were actually to work on the newspaper during their time in Journalism II. The staff members had the job of publishing each edition of the newspaper. They not only researched and wrote the articles, but they were also responsible for the creative design of the newspaper as well as its distribution.

Spectrum had won honors from the Missouri Interscholastic Press Association.[1] Each student received a textbook and would receive a grade in the class. This grade would not depend on whether a student's story was actually published in *Spectrum.*

Three students—Cathy Kuhlmeier, Leslie Smart, and Leanne Tippett—were staff members of *Spectrum* at the time of the censorship. Cathy was a layout editor for *Spectrum,* while Leslie was a newswriter and movie reviewer. Leanne wrote news features, drew cartoons, and was a part-time photographer for the newspaper.

Both the Journalism I and Journalism II classes were taught in accordance with the curriculum guide approved by the school board. This meant that the board approved the course work, assignments, and structure of the class. The curriculum guide described the Journalism II class as a "laboratory situation," and *Spectrum* was the laboratory exercise.[2]

The newspaper was published approximately every three weeks during the 1982–1983 school year, usually six times per semester. During the 1983 school year, more than forty-five hundred copies were distributed to students, school personnel, and members of the local community. Each edition of *Spectrum* contained news about sports and school events and even letters to the editor. A typical edition of *Spectrum* was four pages long.

The February 9, 1985, issue of the St. Louis Globe-Democrat *featured Cathy Kuhlmeier, Leanne Tippett, and Leslie Smart—along with the text of the censored articles.*

Occasionally, however, the staff created a six-page edition if something special was going on at the school, such as homecoming or prom. *Spectrum* sold for twenty-five cents per copy. The proceeds were used to supplement the money *Spectrum* received from the school. Every year, the school board set aside funds in its budget for *Spectrum* to operate. This money helped to cover the various expenses related to producing a school newspaper, such as printing costs and supplies.

The Journalism II course was taught by Robert Stergos for the majority of the 1982–1983 school year. The students met for one fifty-minute period each day. The students also had tasks outside the classroom. After school, they would research topics and investigate possible stories. The amount of work the students did outside of the classroom did not seem to exceed the amount of homework in other classes. As the Journalism II instructor, Stergos advised the staff of the newspaper by giving direction to the students where needed and overseeing the operations of the newspaper. He selected the editor, assistant editor, layout editor, and layout staff. He edited articles and made corrections, often without consulting the staff.[3] He even sold the newspaper from the Journalism II classroom.[4]

In January 1983, Stergos was informed that a copy of each issue of *Spectrum* was to be sent to the principal of Hazelwood East, Ronald Eugene

Reynolds, before it went to the printing company. Stergos did this from January until he left Hazelwood in the spring of 1983. On April 29, 1983, a few weeks before *Spectrum* was censored, Stergos left Hazelwood East for another job. After he left, Howard Emerson took over the job of advising the staff of the newspaper. Emerson was a journalism teacher from Hazelwood Central High School. He began at Hazelwood East High School on May 1, 1983. He was not the substitute for the Journalism II class at that time. The actual substitute, Mrs. Ludwinski, did not have a journalism degree, so the school asked Emerson to assist her by advising the staff of *Spectrum*.[5] Before he left Hazelwood East, Stergos informed Emerson of the directive that he received in January: that *Spectrum* needed to be approved by Reynolds before going to the printer. Emerson did as he was directed and soon found himself involved in a lawsuit after only a short time of being employed at Hazelwood East High School.

Spectrum, May 13 Edition

Howard Emerson received the completed layout of the articles from the students and took notice of the controversial content of a few of the articles. On May 10, Emerson provided Principal Reynolds with the page proofs of the May 13 edition of *Spectrum*. (A page proof is a copy of what the completed edition will look like.) Because he was newly employed, to be safe, Emerson had asked the printer to create two page proofs, one with the controversial articles and one without them. When Emerson did not hear from Reynolds about the May 13 edition, he called him to get his approval. Reynolds read over the May 13 edition while Emerson remained on the line. The phone call lasted approximately twenty minutes. Reynolds was immediately concerned about the content in two of the articles scheduled to appear in that issue. The two articles that Reynolds took issue with appeared on the centerfold of the newspaper on pages 4 and 5 of the page proofs. They appeared under the headline: "Pressure describes it all for today's teenagers: Pregnancy affects many teens each year."

The articles featured on the spread contained other headlines, such as "Teenage Marriages Face 75 Percent Divorce Rate," "Runaways and Juvenile Delinquents Are Common Occurrences in Large Cities," and "Divorce's Impact on Kids May Have Lifelong Effect."

Divorce was becoming a more common issue for school-aged children at that time.[6] Adjusting to a parent's divorce and learning to coexist with step-family members would prove to be difficult for many children. It seemed fitting to the student editors for the school newspaper to address this issue and provide information for students who now found themselves emotionally distraught over their parents' divorce.

However, even though divorce had become more common, discussion about it was not. Factors leading up to a divorce can be complicated and personal. Many families still treated divorce as a very private issue and preferred not to have their family business be a topic of conversation in the school setting.

Shari Gordon was the author of the article written about divorce and its impact on children. The article discussed possible causes of divorce in families and the lifelong aftereffects it can have on children emotionally. It gave statistics and quoted several students' accounts of dealing with divorce in their own families. It contained personal stories by students who had been affected by divorce. One such student was identified as Diane Herbert. In the article, she was quoted as saying that prior to her parents' divorce, her father "was always out of town on business or out late playing cards with the guys" and "wasn't spending enough time with my mom, my sister, and I."[7] Having such details disseminated to the school very well could have upset Diane Herbert's parents.

After the page proof containing these quotes was sent to Reynolds, but before it was sent to publication, Emerson deleted Diane Herbert's name, unbeknownst to the staff of *Spectrum.* Reynolds was concerned that publication of these statements might result in some unhappy parents. Another student, identified only as a junior, was quoted as saying, "My father was an alcoholic and he always came home drunk and my mom really couldn't stand it any longer."[8]

The other article Reynolds was concerned about dealt with an equally controversial topic at that time—teen pregnancy and its ramifications. Recent pregnancies among Hazelwood East students prompted the article in which three pregnant Hazelwood students were interviewed. They discussed their feelings regarding their pregnancies, their relationships with the fathers of their babies, and their plans for the future. Each student was informed that the information they provided would be published in *Spectrum.* Pseudonyms were used for all three girls.

Reynolds felt that the article was inappropriate for a number of reasons. First, he was concerned that the girls might still be identifiable. The newspaper stated, "All names have been changed to keep the identity of these girls a secret."[9] But since there were only a few pregnant students at Hazelwood East, Reynolds thought it would be easy for other students to narrow down and figure out the identities of the interviewees. Second, Reynolds was concerned that the article's content was too mature for the some of the younger students of Hazelwood, as it discussed birth control, sexual activity, and abortion statistics.

With Emerson still on the telephone, Reynolds had to make a decision. Reynolds mistakenly believed that Emerson was at the printer at that very moment, so he was under the impression that an immediate decision had to be made. He did not believe he had enough time to consult with the staff and make the changes that would be necessary in order to make the articles acceptable. Reynolds quickly narrowed down his possible courses of action. He felt he had two options to choose from, and he believed he had to choose quickly. One option would be to wait to publish the newspaper until other articles could be written in place of the two articles he felt were inappropriate. This, however, could cause a great delay in publication and as a result, the students might not be able to publish another edition before the end of the 1983 school year. He knew the students would be upset if this were to happen. The other option would be for Reynolds to act immediately and withdraw the articles he felt were inappropriate. This would mean publishing only a four-page newspaper instead of the planned six-page newspaper.

After reviewing the content of the articles and considering his options, Reynolds decided not to publish the articles dealing with pregnancy and divorce and to delete pages 4 and 5 of the spread entirely. As a result, six articles would be deleted, even though Reynolds objected to only two of them. (The other deleted articles included ones discussing runaways and juvenile delinquency.) After instructing Emerson to have this edition of *Spectrum* published as a four-page newspaper only, Reynolds called and told Dr. Frances Huss, assistant superintendent for secondary education of the school district, about the situation. Dr. Huss agreed with his decision. Reynolds was confident that he had done the right thing in deleting pages 4 and 5.

The May 13 four-page edition of *Spectrum* that did get published contained an article about the recent prom. Another article announced the new selections for the upcoming year's cheerleading squad. Yet another article set forth pointers for summer job hunting for students looking for some extra money during the summer.

Staff members of the newspaper were unaware of the changes that Reynolds had made until the paper was distributed to the student body on May 13. When the students learned that the missing pages had been censored, a group of staff members decided to confront Reynolds about his decision. When they met with Reynolds and inquired about the changes made to the newspaper, he stated that some material was deleted because it was too sensitive for some of the younger students at

Hazelwood. He went on to explain his concern about the anonymity of the students in the teen pregnancy article. The staff of *Spectrum* was far from satisfied by his answers because *Spectrum* had, in the past, published articles that discussed teenage marriage and teenage pregnancy.

On May 16, a notice was posted by the school administration in the journalism room of the school. It read:

> The content of some of the articles were *personal* and highly sensitive—people and names were used.
>
> The information was sensitive and totally unnecessary to be included in the school newspaper.
>
> They have many other opportunities to achieve goals in journalism class or publishing of the school newspaper that do not require that kind of reporting.
>
> Learning can take place in research and reporting that is less sensitive, less controversial, and certainly something that is just as beneficial to the students.[10]

At that point, members of *Spectrum*'s staff contacted the American Civil Liberties Union (ACLU) of Eastern Missouri looking for legal advice.

The Students Contact the ACLU

The ACLU is a non-profit organization that fights to defend the rights of people as outlined in the Bill of Rights, the first ten amendments to the United States

Constitution. The ACLU fights in court, in Congress, and in communities. It has members all over the country who are all united in the primary goal of protecting the constitutional rights of every American by assuring that Bill of Rights amendments to the Constitution are preserved. Members fight to protect freedom of religion, freedom of speech, freedom of the press, and freedom of assembly, all as outlined in the First Amendment:

> Congress shall make no law respecting an establishment of religion, or prohibiting the free exercise thereof; or abridging the freedom of speech, or of the press; or the right of the people peaceably to assemble, and to petition the government for a redress of grievances.

The ACLU also fights to ensure that every citizen be treated equally, regardless of their age, gender, national origin, or religion, and that each person's rights be respected when being deprived of life, liberty, or property.

The Hazelwood East students would now begin a journey that would propel them into the national spotlight. Would they prevail? Were they in over their heads? In May 1983, members of the *Spectrum* staff were prepared to fight for their right of expression in their school newspaper—but were they prepared to stand up for their rights all the way to the Supreme Court of the United States?

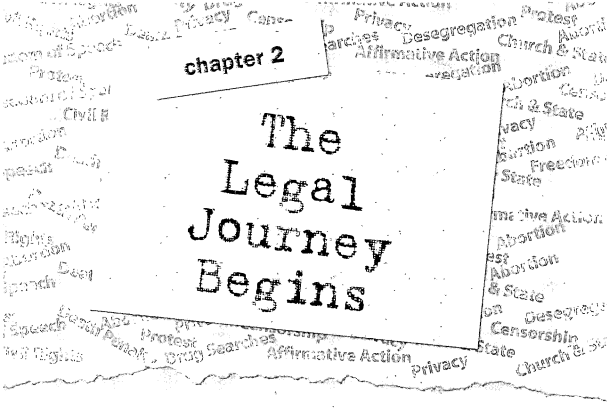

chapter 2

The Legal Journey Begins

Local chapters of the ACLU often have paid staff attorneys working in their offices. Sometimes, volunteer attorneys assist in giving legal advice to people who feel that their constitutional rights may have been violated. Cathy Kuhlmeier, Leanne Tippett, and Leslie Smart were assigned to one such volunteer, Leslie D. Edwards of the Eastern Missouri chapter. A staff attorney, Stephen Miller III, was also assigned to the case.

With the help of these two attorneys, a lawsuit was filed in the United States District Court for the Eastern District of Missouri on August 19, 1983, which named the three girls as plaintiffs. Plaintiffs are the people bringing a lawsuit who claim that they have suffered harm in some way. It can be physical harm, financial harm, or, as in this case, harm through denial of constitutional rights. Defendants are the people or entities against whom a lawsuit is filed. This lawsuit was filed against Hazelwood School District and several members of the faculty and school board. The lawsuit asked the judge presiding over the case, John F. Nangle, Chief Judge for the Eastern District of Missouri, to force the school to publish the censored articles. It asked that the court find *Spectrum* to be a public forum for free expression by students. The lawsuit alleged that since the newspaper was a public forum for expression, the staff members of the newspaper were protected by the First Amendment. It also claimed that the students should be compensated financially for the violation of their constitutional rights.

All three girls had graduated from Hazelwood East by the time the trial began. Cathy and Leslie had been juniors and Leanne had been a senior during the 1983 school year when the censorship took place. The story had received press coverage within the community.[1] This was a story of interest.

At the trial, Hazelwood East was represented by Robert P. Baine, Jr. He had prepared members of the school board and faculty for the trial. Reynolds and Emerson were called to testify, as were the three students, numerous teachers at Hazelwood East, and two expert witnesses. The case was tried before Judge Nangle. No jury was present during the trial. Parties in a lawsuit can choose to present their case to a judge without a jury. This is known as a bench trial.

During his testimony, Reynolds reiterated the concerns he had previously stated in May 1983. He mentioned his concern for the anonymity of the pregnant girls interviewed for the article on teen pregnancy. He also said he had been concerned for the fathers of the babies and their rights to privacy. He testified that he felt some of the material was not suitable for younger Hazelwood students because

Leslie Edwards, on the left, was a volunteer attorney with the ACLU. Here she meets with Leanne Tippett (center) and Leslie Smart (right) to discuss the case.

birth control, abortion, and sexual activity were mentioned in the articles. He also testified regarding his concern for the divorced parents mentioned in the articles: They had not given their permission for personal facts regarding their marriages to be published, nor were they given the opportunity to rebut the statements made by their children.

Reynolds also said that he had been forced to act quickly. Even though he did not find everything on the two-page spread inappropriate, he said, he believed that he did not have the time to make only certain modifications to the articles regarding divorce and teen pregnancy. He testified that he felt it was reasonable, given the time constraint, to delete the entire two-page spread, even though some of the articles did not have inappropriate content. Reynolds was confident he made the right decision given the circumstances.

The school district had Martin Duggan testify as an expert witness. He had been a college journalism instructor and supervised a college newspaper. He stated that journalists need to present all sides of an issue. He stated that some people mentioned in the articles were not given a chance to respond, and thus all sides of the issues were not being relayed to the reader. He also distinguished the difference between censorship and editing. He stated that censorship comes from an outside source, whereas editing is from an internal source.

Legal Terms

amicus curiae (plural, amici curiae)—Literally, "friend of the court"; someone who files a brief in a case in which that person is not a party but has a strong interest. Such briefs let the court benefit from the added viewpoint.

appeal—A request to review a lower court's decision.

appellate court (sometimes called a court of appeals)—A court that reviews decisions of lower courts for fairness and accuracy. An appellate court can reverse a lower court's ruling.

appellant or petitioner—The person who thinks the lower court made an error.

appellee or respondent—The person who won the case in the lower court.

brief—Written statement of a party's argument on one or more issues in the case.

concur—To agree with the ruling in a court case.

defendant—In a civil case, any person or entity named in a lawsuit. In a criminal case, any person charged with a crime.

dissent—To disagree with the ruling in a court case.

majority opinion—The ruling and reasoning supported by a majority of appellate court judges in a case. **Concurring opinions** are written by judges who agree with the majority holding but have other reasons for their views. **Dissenting opinions** are written by judges who disagree with the ruling.

precedent—A legal holding that will determine how courts decide future cases.

testimony—Statements made under oath.

writ of certiorari (ser-she-o-RAR-ee)—A decision by the Supreme Court to hear a decision from a lower court.

The students' expert witness was Robert P. Knight, a college professor of journalism. He told the court that he felt the articles were neither defamatory nor obscene, that they complied with recognized journalism standards, and that they would not cause a disruption of the educational environment. It was revealed that in 1983 Dr. Knight had given a lecture at a national convention of investigative reporters and asked those attending to support the students in this lawsuit. Testimony from both experts was considered, but Duggan's was given more weight because the court determined that he was more objective than Dr. Knight.

Judge Nangle handed down a verdict in the case on May 9, 1985, two years after the censorship took place. The court found in favor of the defendant, Hazelwood School District, finding that *Spectrum* was not a public forum subject to free expression by students. (In referring to legal decisions, the terms "court" and "judge" are often used interchangeably.) The court had come to the conclusion, based on the evidence, that Hazelwood had not violated the constitutional rights of the students. The court found Reynolds's concerns regarding privacy to be legitimate and reasonable. Given the fact that there were approximately eight to ten pregnant teenage students at Hazelwood East at that time, the court agreed that it might not be difficult to discern the identity of the three students interviewed based on certain facts given during the interviews, such as expected delivery dates.

The students had testified that they were under the impression they could publish practically anything in *Spectrum.* Evidence was presented during the trial that previous issues of *Spectrum* had published articles discussing controversial and sensitive issues such as teenage pregnancy, cults, and students' use of drugs and alcohol.[2] The court did not find the students' testimony regarding their impression of their freedom to publish practically anything to be credible. With the amount of oversight Stergos had prior to his departure, the court found that the staff of *Spectrum* could not reasonably have thought they had free rein to publish anything they liked.[3]

The court held that the school could impose restraints on the students' speech in activities that are integral to the school's educational function. It further found that the publication of the school newspaper created by the Journalism II class was an activity that was integral to the school's educational function. The court stated that the Journalism II class was much like other classes held at Hazelwood East during that school year. The students enrolled in Journalism II were required to attend class on a daily basis. Therefore, participating in *Spectrum* was not like playing a sport or participating in extracurricular activities for the school, the court reasoned. The court was not swayed by evidence presented indicating that Stergos had received extra money both for his services as coach of the baseball team and for his services in connection with *Spectrum*.[4] This fact alone did not demonstrate to the court that Stergos's services with the extracurricular baseball team were comparable to his services with *Spectrum*. (The defense had argued that Stergos was only compensated for his travel time to and from the printing company, since he drove his own vehicle.)

The court did, however, place one restraint on the school. It required the school to have a reasonable basis for its decision to censor material in school activities. What constituted such a basis? What may seem reasonable to one person may not seem reasonable to another. How would "reasonable" be defined? Ultimately, the court agreed with Reynolds and held that his concern for the pregnant students' anonymity and the privacy of the divorced parents were reasonable motivational factors for censoring the school newspaper. The court also found that Reynolds was justified in his concern that the articles were too mature for younger students at Hazelwood.

It was a total loss for the plaintiffs. The court had decided that given the nature of the articles

Reynolds had received and the deadline that he believed he faced, censorship was a reasonable response.

The Students Appeal

When a civil trial verdict is handed down in federal court, the losing side may appeal to the Court of Appeals. The three girls decided to do just that. They would take this case to the next level. They appealed the decision of the District Court and soon found the case in front of the Court of Appeals for the Eighth Circuit. Judges Gerald Heaney, Roger Wollman, and Richard Arnold would hear the case.

On July 7, 1986, Judge Heaney for the Court of Appeals issued the court's decision in this case. It had decided to reverse the lower court's ruling. This was wonderful news for the students. When a higher court reverses a lower court's ruling, it is stating that the lower court was incorrect in its decision. The Court of Appeals disagreed entirely with the lower court. It held that *Spectrum* was indeed a public forum subject to free expression by students. Because the students created the newspaper, wrote the articles, and designed the layout, the court held that it was a "student publication." The court referenced the "Statement of Policy" that was published at the beginning of each school year in *Spectrum,* which read in part:

> *Spectrum* is a school funded newspaper; written, edited, and designed by members of the Journalism II class with assistance of advisor Mr. Robert Stergos. *Spectrum* follows journalism guidelines that are set by *Scholastic Journalism* textbook. . . . *Spectrum*, as a student-press publication, accepts all rights implied by the First Amendment of the United States Constitution which states that: "Congress shall make no law restricting . . . or abridging the freedom of speech or the press. . . ." That this right extends to high school students was clarified in the *Tinker* vs. *Des Moines Community School District* case in 1969.[5]

The policy statement further said that the articles and editorials reflected the view of the staff of *Spectrum* and not that of the administrators or faculty of the high school.

The appeals court found that because *Spectrum* was a public forum, the students were entitled to some First Amendment protection. The court applied the rule stated in *Tinker* v. *Des Moines Community School District,* which held that in a high school setting, school officials must demonstrate that a restriction was necessary to avoid material and substantial interference with schoolwork or discipline. In *Tinker,* the Supreme Court had ruled that Iowa public school officials violated the First Amendment rights of several students by suspending them for wearing black armbands to school to protest the United States' involvement in Vietnam. It held that students do not "shed their constitutional rights to freedom of speech or expression at the schoolhouse gate."[6] The Court found that the students were wearing the armbands as a form of symbolic speech. It rejected the school officials' argument that the armbands would disrupt the school environment. The Court held:

> The principle use to which the schools are dedicated is to accommodate students during prescribed hours for the purpose of certain types of activities. Among those activities is personal intercommunication among the students. This is not only an inevitable part of the process of attending school; it is also an important part of the educational process. A student's rights, therefore, do not embrace merely the classroom hours. When he is in the cafeteria, or on the playing field, or on the campus during the authorized hours, he may express his opinions, even on controversial subjects like the conflict in Vietnam, if he does so without "materially and substantially interfer[ing] with the requirements of appropriate discipline in the operation of the school" and without colliding with the rights of others.[7]

The Court stated that fear of a disturbance is not enough to overcome the right to freedom of expression. School officials must be able to reasonably predict that student speech will cause a substantial interference with school activities or that it will invade the rights of others before they can censor student expression.

The Court of Appeals found no evidence that Reynolds could have reasonably predicted that any

Cathy Kuhlmeier holds a copy of Spectrum, *the school newspaper that was censored by the principal because he objected to some of the articles.*

of the material in the deleted articles would have disrupted classwork or caused disorder in the school. Therefore, the court reasoned, the articles should not have been censored. If privacy was the main concern for the school, it could only censor the newspaper if it could demonstrate that the school could have been sued for invasion of privacy or for libel, the act of harming someone's reputation by printing false information about them. The school district was unable to convince the court that it could have been sued if it had left the May 13 edition of *Spectrum* intact. The students came out victorious. However, the victory would not last long.

The very same day, the Supreme Court of the United States issued a decision that held that public school officials could limit the speech of students. It was the case of *Bethel School District No. 403* v. *Fraser.* The Supreme Court ruled that the First Amendment did not prohibit schools from punishing vulgar and lewd speech since such speech was not consistent with fundamental values of public school education. In this case, Matthew Fraser, a student at Bethel High School in Bethel, Washington, had made a speech nominating a fellow student for student government. In his speech, Fraser used sexually explicit language to promote the candidacy of his friend. Students reacted to the comments—some were embarrassed, while others yelled and cheered. Fraser was suspended from school for two days. The Court held that even though the First Amendment protects the use of offensive expression by adults, this protection did not extend to children in a public school setting.

This is just what the school district needed: a ruling by the Supreme Court that seemed to state clearly that public schools could limit the speech of their students. They asked the Court of Appeals for the Eighth Circuit to reconsider its reversal by way of rehearing the case. This request was denied. Would the school district appeal to the Supreme Court of the United States? If so, would the Supreme Court decide to hear the case?

Hazelwood Appeals to the Supreme Court

The only thing left for the school district to do was to go to the court of last resort. The school district could file a petition for writ of certiorari, which basically asks the Supreme Court of the United States to hear its case. The decision of the nine justices is final. The Court generally follows a "rule of four": If four justices agree that a case should be heard, the case will be placed on the Supreme Court's docket and an order stating that certiorari has been granted is issued to the petitioner.

Thousands of cases are appealed to the Supreme Court each year. However, the Court chooses a very small number of cases to hear— usually between ninety and one hundred cases. Typically, the cases chosen involve interesting and controversial issues. The lower trial and appellate courts may be interpreting a certain rule of law or prior court decision in very different ways. The Supreme Court may choose a case so it can offer guidance in the interpretation of the law and set the standard for the lower trial and appellate courts to follow.

On January 20, 1987, the Supreme Court granted certiorari. The parties in the litigation would soon find themselves in the national spotlight. Rights of public school students throughout the nation were hanging in the balance. In the quest to fight for the right to publish the entire May 13 edition of *Spectrum,* three young women who had started this journey nearly four years earlier now found themselves fighting for the rights of all American public school students. This lawsuit was about to reach the final and most important stage yet.

The Case for the School District

The attorneys for the school district immediately began to prepare for the oral arguments that would take place before the Supreme Court. Robert P. Baine, Jr., would argue the case with the help of John Gianoulakis and Robert T. Haar.

The lawyers began to work on their legal briefs. A brief is a written compilation of the arguments that will be presented to the Court. The appellant (the party bringing the lawsuit to the Supreme Court) and the appellee (the party responding to the lawsuit) exchange legal briefs well before the arguments are heard by the justices. The party petitioning the court can then submit a reply brief which addresses the issues raised in their opponents' brief. Exchanging briefs gives each party an opportunity to get a peek at the arguments that opposing counsel will be making to the justices. Each party can then try to expand their arguments to rebut the claims made by the other side.

The arguments took place in a session before the eight justices of the Supreme Court. At that time, former Chief Justice Lewis Powell had retired. President Ronald Reagan had nominated Robert Bork to be an associate justice, but the Senate had not confirmed his nomination. As a result, only eight justices would hear this case, not the usual nine. This could cause a split decision of four votes for each side. If this occurred, the Court of Appeals decision would stand, and the school district would lose.

The appellate brief submitted by Baine set forth the facts of the case. The school district was trying to persuade the justices to find that Leslie Edwards, attorney for the students, was incorrect in her application of the law and that the Court of Appeals had ruled incorrectly. It discussed ways that past decisions by the Supreme Court related to their case. The brief pointed to prior rulings by the Supreme Court in which the Court had held that school authorities could control certain speech in school. The attorneys had to try to draw as many similarities as possible between their case and those past cases. The brief and the argument needed to be persuasive.

The first legal issue the attorneys addressed was the concept of a public forum. They argued that the Court of Appeals had erred when it found *Spectrum* to be a public forum. The Supreme Court had to decide whether or not *Spectrum* was a public forum by determining if the students worked on *Spectrum* solely for the purposes of communicating their beliefs and ideas. If so, that would support the argument that *Spectrum* was a public forum subject to First Amendment protection.

A traditional public forum has a history of freedom of expression. Places considered traditional public forums include public parks, public streets, sidewalks, or similar areas that have traditionally been considered places for free communication. The government cannot restrict the content of speech in a public forum unless it can show that the restriction is necessary to further a compelling government interest. This means that the government must have an important reason for the restriction. The government is only permitted to control the time the speech can occur and how it will occur. The school district argued that since *Spectrum* was not open to the public for communication, it was not a traditional public forum.

Another type of public forum is a limited public forum. This is a place that can sometimes be used for people to express beliefs but often is used for purposes not related to expression. The forum can be opened for expressive activity for a certain amount of time, certain groups, or certain topics. Examples of limited public forums are a state university meeting room, a municipal auditorium, or a theater owned by a city. The government cannot restrict expression in a limited forum unless that restriction serves a compelling governmental interest.

Because each edition of *Spectrum* was subject to the final approval of a school official regarding article content, length, and layout, the school district claimed it could not be considered a public forum or limited public forum. The attorneys focused on the fact that *Spectrum* was the laboratory assignment for the Journalism II class. Work on the newspaper was intended to supplement the information students had learned while enrolled in Journalism I. Working on the newspaper would give the students hands-on experience with the production of a newspaper. It would allow the students an opportunity to get acquainted with deadlines, information-gathering techniques, and the actual production of a newspaper. If the Supreme Court upheld the decision of the Court of Appeals, the attorneys argued, the Journalism II teacher and *Spectrum* advisor would not have the ability to edit the newspaper at all without proving there was a compelling governmental interest behind the edit.

Spectrum Is Not a Public Forum as Defined by the Law

The school district claimed that since *Spectrum* was neither a public forum nor a limited public forum, the decision by Reynolds to delete the entire two-page spread did not need to have a compelling governmental purpose. Thus, the students did not have First Amendment protection in the school-sponsored newspaper. Therefore, the school district argued, Reynolds did not have to prove that he had no other alternative than to do what he did. They said he had the right to control the content of the school-sponsored newspaper, and so his actions were justified. They claimed that Reynolds's concerns about privacy, as well as his concern that some of the material was too mature for some students, were reasonable in the circumstances.

The Court of Appeals had found that the article on teenage pregnancy by Shari Gordon was informative, considering that teen pregnancy had become an issue at Hazelwood East, with eight to ten students pregnant at the time. The school district argued that the lower court was incorrect in its response to the teen pregnancy article; it claimed the court had misapplied the law by coming to that conclusion. The district asked the Supreme Court to apply the holding in the recent *Bethel* v. *Fraser* decision, in which the Court had held that school officials can act in place of parents to protect

Principal Ronald Reynolds made the decision to censor several articles scheduled to appear in Spectrum. *He believed they violated students' privacy and contained material that was inappropriate for younger students.*

students. It is the job of the school officials, the school district argued, to decide what is acceptable expression by students. If the school officials felt the material was too sensitive for some of the younger students, then the school officials should have been given the latitude to be the final decision maker on the issue without legal ramifications.

The school district emphasized the numerous objections Reynolds had regarding the privacy rights of others mentioned in the articles, focusing on the article that contained student quotes regarding their parents' divorces. The school district felt it was not appropriate to print such statements without notifying the parents or allowing them to rebut the statements. They also noted that they were concerned that the school could be sued by some of the people mentioned in the articles because they had not consented to have statements about them published. The school district also noted that Reynolds was concerned that the articles concerning pregnancy and birth control would give the impression to the students and the public that the school endorsed the sexual behaviors that were discussed in the articles. They claimed that Reynolds's concern was reasonable given the maturity level of some students of high school age.

The attorneys for the district also pointed out the time constraints that Reynolds was under when he made the decision to the delete the articles. They argued that his decision to delete the entire two-page spread was reasonable given his impressions of the deadline. Reynolds believed that if he made changes only to the articles with which he took issue, the last edition of *Spectrum* might not be printed at all.

Reynolds Made a Reasonable Decision to Censor *Spectrum*

The attorneys for the Hazelwood school district focused on the word "reasonable." They argued that even if the Supreme Court agreed with the Appeals Court and found in favor of the students, the Court of Appeals had incorrectly applied the law. The Court of Appeals had applied the *Tinker* test, which required the school to find that the material invaded the rights of others or would substantially disrupt the school before they could censor the material. Attorneys for the school district claimed the test was not whether the material would substantially disrupt the school but whether the school's concerns were reasonable given the circumstances. Under that reasonableness test, they argued, the school district had the right to delete inappropriate content from the school-sponsored newspaper.

National Interest in the Case

When a case goes before the Supreme Court, it is a big deal because the outcome of the case will usually have long-reaching effects. Many people or organizations within the country can have a stake in the outcome. Interest in this case extended beyond the borders of Missouri because it would affect the rights of students throughout the country. Because of this, the Supreme Court may allow interested people or organizations who are not parties to the case to submit legal briefs on the issue and sometimes even argue their positions. Such a person or organization is known as an *amicus curiae,* which is Latin for "friend of the court." The National School Boards Association, the Pacific Legal Foundation, and the School Board of Dade County, Florida, filed *amicus curiae* briefs urging the Supreme Court to reverse the decision of the Court of Appeals and find in favor of the school district.

Baine Argues the Case

Robert Baine presented his case and fielded numerous questions from the eight justices.[1] What was the purpose of *Spectrum*? Was it merely a laboratory assignment? These were the types of questions asked of Baine. He again argued his position that *Spectrum* was a laboratory assignment for the students and as such was under the control of the school officials. Would five justices agree with Baine? Would they find Reynolds acted reasonably under the circumstances? The students now had their chance to present their case. Would they sway the justices to find in their favor?

The Case for the Students

The school district had presented its case. Now it was time to hear from Leslie Edwards, the attorney for the students. She too submitted an appellate brief to the Court. It claimed that the school had violated the students' constitutional rights.

Like most attorneys, Edwards and Baine had never argued in front of the Supreme Court. This was an opportunity of a lifetime. In actuality, only a small percentage of lawyers in the country have the opportunity to argue in front of the Supreme Court. Since the Court only hears a small percentage of cases, the likelihood of an attorney getting the chance to argue in front of the nine justices is not great. To argue in front of the Supreme Court, an attorney must be sponsored by two members of the Bar of the Supreme Court. They must also pay a fee and prove to the Court that they were admitted to practice in the highest court in a state for at least three years and that they have not been disciplined in the last three years.

The First School Newspaper

Edwards began her argument by discussing the first documented school newspaper in history. On June 11, 1777, four students began publishing a school newspaper at Penn Charter School in Philadelphia, ten years before the Constitution and before the addition of the First Amendment.[1] It was called the *Students Gazette,* and it was sold in exchange for a scrap of paper.[2] The students reported on news of interest to the school community. Even before the Constitution, Edwards argued, the concept of a student newspaper was seen as important.

Edwards then turned her attention to the 1983 *Spectrum.* She argued that *Spectrum* was not just a laboratory assignment, as the school district argued. She said that *Spectrum* was a student newspaper and as such, the staff should receive the same protections as journalists outside the school setting. The fact that the staff of *Spectrum* worked on the newspaper while attending school did not make them any less deserving of First Amendment protection, Edwards argued.

The school officials, she said, should not have editorial control over the students' views. Once the school censored an item based on the viewpoint or an idea that was expressed, the school violated the students' First Amendment rights, according to Edwards. Asked by one of the justices if she thought that it was possible to have an effective journalism class that produced a newspaper where the school maintained control over all aspects of that publication, including content, Edwards replied, "I think that when you get student expression involved, then the school's control can not be activated."[3] Could Edwards convince the justices that the school district edited the May 13 edition of *Spectrum* not because it was controlling the curriculum of the Journalism II class, but because it was controlling the views and expression of the students?

Spectrum Is a Limited Public Forum as Defined by Law

Edwards argued that *Spectrum* was a limited public forum. It was a school newspaper. Hazelwood East was a public school open to the students who are enrolled and to the families and friends of the students. When a special event took place at the school, members of the community were invited to attend. The newspaper was the product of the students of Hazelwood East, but access to the paper was open to the public. Students, faculty, and members of the community purchased editions of *Spectrum* to read. It contained a section entitled "Letters to the Editor," where contributions were welcome from students. Edwards argued, and the Court of Appeals had agreed, that given *Spectrum*'s many contacts with the local community, the newspaper was a limited public forum entitled to First Amendment protection.

Edwards argued that the Journalism I and II classes were aimed at teaching students the fundamentals of journalism and reporting. She pointed out that every professional journalist is aware of the protections of the Constitution and in our society, newspaper journalists have First Amendment protection. If we lived in a society where journalists did not have this protection, she asked, would we receive accurate reporting? Would the lack of protection cause journalists to shy away from controversial stories? Edwards acknowledged that the students in the Journalism II class needed an advisor. They needed a person with journalism experience to guide them through the publication of the newspaper. She argued, however, that the advisor could guide the staff of *Spectrum* without controlling the views expressed in the newspaper.

Pressure describes it all
Pregnancy affects many

by Andree Callow

Sixteen year old Sue had it all—good looks, good grades, a loving family and a cute boyfriend. She also had a seven pound baby boy. Each year, according to Claire Berman (Readers Digest May 1983), close to 1.1 million teenagers—more than one out of every ten teenage girls—become pregnant. In Missouri alone, 8,208 teens under the age of 18, became pregnant in 1980, according to Reproductive Health Services of St. Louis. That number was 7,363 in 1981.

Unplanned pregnancies can no longer be dismissed as something that only happens to disadvantaged teen sfrom lower social-economic groups. In fact, the highest rise in out-of-wedlock births has been among 15 to 17 year old whites, according to Claire Berman. Thirty percent of births out-of-wedlock in Missouri were to young white mothers and 89 percent were to young mothers of other races.

Teenage sexuality Y:
Other statistics connected with teenage pregnancy are equally noteworthy. The rate of teenage sexual activity in the U.S. is alarmingly high. Of every teenager in the country, between the ages of 13 and 19, seven million teenage boys and five million teenage girls are sexually active, according to a study done by the Alan Guttmacher Institute, which specializes in family planning. According to the national average, teenagers begin sexual activity at about age 16.

Birth control : Nearly, two-thirds of sexually active teenagers do not use birth control. If birth control is used, it is used irregularly. The 62 percent who have never used birth control run a high risk of getting pregnant. "I've had many a girl tell me she gave her pills to a friend because she wouldn't be needing them herself that week", says a nurse who works with pregnant teens (Readers Digest, May 1983). "When sex education is offered, it too often is confined to diagrams of the uterus and ovary. A lot of kids have seen a lot of diagrams. What they don't know is sex can lead to babies!"

Even with the availability of birth control, many teens experiment with sex for months before using contraceptives. "It's as if being prepared makes one immoral," says Linda Nessel, who is associated with the Pregnant Teen, Teen Mother program at New York's YMCA. "These girls believe that if you plan for sex, you're fast or bad. So it's the 'good' girls who get pregnant."

Although peer pressure plays a large role in unintended pregnancies, ignorance seems to play the largest part. "In spite of their sexual experience, these youngsters lack in information," says Naomi Berman, who is also associated with the YMCA program. "They don't know such basic facts about their bodies as when conception is likely to occur and they're afraid to ask questions for fear of appearing dumb."

Mom and dad Parents should discuss sex with their children, talking about emotions as well as actions, making their children aware of the parental standing and the reason for them, according to Claire Berman.

However, 98 percent of our countries parents say they feel uncomfortable and need help in discussing sex with their own children, says Planned Parenthood Affiliates of Missouri.

Sex-education specialist, Ruth MacDonald, urges that parents learn to talk more ever ten abortions were obtained by teenagers.

A major problem in teenage abortions is teenagers delay having their abortions, thereby increasing risks to health by as much as 100 percent for every week delayed, says Planned Parenthood.

Although most teenagers choose abortion, says Claire Berman, there are still three live births for every five abortions.

Consequences CES: The consequences of teenage teenage childbearing is the interruption of schooling. Teenage mothers who give birth before the age of 18 are only half as likely to graduate from high school as teens who put off childbearing until their 20's. Teenage fathers who are under the age of 18 at the birth of their babies are two-fifth as likely to graduate from high school as those who aren't fathers yet.

Teenage pregnancy is becoming an epidemic. It has become a major health, social, and economic problem for this country. Millions of teens get

TEEN ABORTIONS, 1976-1980

AGE	1976	1977	1978	1979	1980
Total	13,869	14,762	17,785	21,267	21,671
Under 15	237	256	250	293	263
15-17	1,945	2,239	2,694	3,071	2,976
18-19	2,498	2,547	2,986	3,800	3,767

Obtained from the Missouri Association of Planned Parenthood Affiliates, Inc.

comfortably about the subject, because their children are surrounded by it. "Parents can't stop kids from listening to music or watching television," she says, "but they have to realize they are still the most important force in their children's lives—and that they have to get equal time with the other influences. This is a whole new society."

Abortion : Between the ... ... there was a 51 percent increase in teenage abortions, according to Planned Parenthood. In 1980, three out of pregnancy are alarming. The risk of death to babies born of teenage mothers is nearly two times greater than the risk to babies born of women in their 20's, according to Planned Parenthood. Teenagers are more likely to have premature birth and 23 percent more gikely to suffer complications related to premature births. Teenagers also have a 39 percent greater risk of having a baby of low birth weight, a major cause of infant deaths, illnesses, and defects.

Another consequence of pregnant each year and millions will in years to come. Could one of them be you?

Squeal law
by Christine De Hass
The squeal rule was proposed by the Health and Human Services Department to help prevent teenage pregnancy and to strengthen the communication bond between parents and their daughters, making teenage sexuality a family matter.

The rule would require

This shows the top half of the two-page spread that was removed from the May 13 edition of Spectrum *on instructions from Principal Reynolds.*

for today's teenagers

teens each year

notification to parents within ten days of the time their daughter, under 18, received birth control pills, a diaphragm or an IUD from a federally-funded clinic.

Nationwide, the rule would affect around 5,100 clinics and over 500,000 minors who receive prescriptions from these clinics each year.

Proponents of the rule have brought figures into focus saying that the use of contraceptives by teenagers is dangerous to their health, but the statistics were obtained from women over 30 who smoke.

Planned Parenthood, which could lose $30 million in federal subsidies by promising confidentiality to prescribers, introduced facts which prove that not the use of contraceptives, but being pregnant itself, is the riskier for teens. The statistics say that, for every 100,000 teenagers who give birth to live babies, approximately 11 girls die, as told to Amity Shlaes of "The New Republic."

Ms. Shlaes also pointed out another factor. "In a family where the child has already chosen to have sex without telling her parents, how will a letter in the mail announcing the fact improve family relations?"

Proponents argue that a girl who uses contraceptives and goes to a clinic is showing responsible actions. By putting the rule into effect, it would put girls down for their actions.

Proponents say that the rule would decrease pregnancies if put into effect. However, experts say that if the rule was put into effect, teenage pregnancies would increase up to 100,000 a year. For all points, the rule is out of date in a world where male contraceptives are available at the local drug store.

To the satisfaction of the rule's opponents, a federal judge disallowed the government from putting the rule into effect by issuing a permanent injunction against it in early March.

Mrs. Barbara Bughman, nurse at East, would not agree or disagree with the judge's decision. "I can see both sides. There are cases where it would be beneficial. I can't say whether it's right or wrong. It's an individual thing."

Introduction

These stories are the personal accounts of three Hazelwood East students who became pregnant. All names have been changed to keep the identity of these girls a secret.

Terri:

I am five months pregnant and very excited about having my baby. My husband is excited too. We both can't wait until it's born.

After the baby is born, which is in July, we are planning to move out of his house, when we save enough money. I am not going to be coming back to school right away (September) because the baby will only be

two months old. I plan on coming back in January when the second semester begins.

When I first found out I was pregnant, I really was kind of shocked because I kept thinking about how I was going to tell my parents. I was also real happy. I just couldn't believe I was going to have a baby. When I told Paul about the situation, he was really happy. At first I didn't think he would be because I wasn't sure if he really would want to take on the responsibility of being a father, but he was very happy. We talked about the baby and what we were going to do and we both wanted to get married. We had talked about marriage before, so we were both sure of what we were doing.

I had no pressures (to have sex). It was my own decision. We were going out four or five months before we had sex. I was on no kind of birth control pills. I really didn't want to get them, not just so I could get pregnant. I don't think I'd feel right taking them.

At first my parents were upset, especially my father, but now they're both happy for me. I don't have any regrets because I'm happy about the baby and I hope everything works out.

Patti:

I didn't think it could happen to me, but I knew I had to start making plans for me and my little one. I think Steven (my boyfriend (was more scared than me. He was away at college and when he came home we cried together and then accepted it.

At first both families were disappointed, but the third or fourth month, when the baby started to kick, and move around, my boyfriend and I felt like expecting parents and we were very excited!

My parents really like my boyfriend. At first we all felt sort of uncomfortable around each other. Now my boyfriends supports our baby totally (except fo███ ng) and my parents ███ really does love us, s███ ppy. Her I graduate███ar, we're getting marri███ I can talk t███her about anything but███t face her and tell h███egnant. I never th███happen to me.

My ███ I have a beaut███ip and it's been th███since three years ag███e, I really do think ███ture looks good for b███).

Steven t███ of my baby. We have a ███ount for hi██ (baby) and ███e's away at school I get ███ut as I ne███ it.

I want to s███thers th███ isn't easy and███es a str███g, willing pers███ handle it because it do███n giving up a lot of thi███econdly, if you're no███o give your child all███nd affection around, ███ be a good parent. Lastly, be careful because the pill doesn't always work. I know because it didn't work for me.

This experience has made me a more responsible person. I feel that now I am a woman. If I could go back to last year, I would not get pregnant, but I

have no regrets. We love our baby more than anything in the world (my boyfriend and I) could we fmt love him??? . . . he's so cute and innocent . . .

Julie:

At first I was shocked. You always think "It won't happen to me". I was also scared because I did not know how everyone was going to handle it. But the, I started getting excited.

There was never really any pressure (to have sex), it was more of a mutual agreement. I think I was more curious than anything.

I had always planned on continuing school. There was never any doubt about that. I found that it wasn't as hard as I thought it would be. I was fairly open about it and people seemed to accept it. Greg and I did not get married. We figured that those were ███ the best circumstances,███ we decided to wait and ███e how things go. We ███re st███ planning on getting mar███d when we are financi███ ready.███also am planning ███oing to c███ge a███east part of ███me.

My paren███ ███ great. They ███ot have ███more ███e and help███. They ███ng everything t███ can f███s and enjoy being "gran-d███a and grandpa". They have also made it clear it was my responsibility.

My parents (especially my mom) are willing to talk about sex, but I always feel very uncomfortable. I guess you never think about your parents doing things like that. An older

The Censorship Did Not Serve a Governmental Interest

Edwards argued that because *Spectrum* was a limited public forum, the rule in *Tinker* needed to be applied to the case. Under *Tinker,* the school district would have to demonstrate to the Court that there was a compelling governmental interest in deleting material from the May 13 edition of *Spectrum.* Edwards pointed to the fact that the school district could not show that the articles would disrupt the school environment. She said the school merely found the content to be inappropriate. The school district officials claimed to have concerns about the privacy rights of the divorced parents and the fathers of the babies mentioned in the articles. But, she asked, did these concerns really rise to the level of a compelling government interest? Even if an issue was raised by one of the third parties mentioned in the articles, would this disrupt the school environment? Edwards argued that it would not. She argued that the school district's concern really came down to morals, disapproval of the topics, and viewpoints of the articles.

Edwards argued to the Court that what constituted "inappropriate" was a subjective standard, open to interpretation. Allowing a *Spectrum* advisor to censor what he felt was inappropriate would allow him to make a judgment based on viewpoint and this, Edwards claimed, was a violation of the Constitution. If the Supreme Court allowed this type of control by this school board, how would students across the country approach their schools' newspapers?

Would they be given guidelines as to what constituted "appropriate" content? How would they know what was acceptable and appropriate journalism? Would students steer clear of all controversial topics for fear of negative repercussions? Edwards compared the case at hand to another Supreme Court case that dealt with viewpoint censorship: *Board of Education, Island Trees Union Free School District* v. *Pico*. This case involved five students who filed a lawsuit in federal court when the school board, without notice to the school librarian or students, removed nine books from the school libraries. The school board characterized the books as "anti-American, anti-Christian, anti-Semitic, and just plain filthy."[4] The students argued that their First Amendment rights were violated when the school denied them access to the books. The Supreme Court agreed with the students and held that school boards may not remove books from school library shelves simply because they do not approve of the ideas contained in those books. The Court did acknowledge that school boards do have the power to manage the schools. However, the Court asserted, the school boards' discretion needed to be exercised in a manner consistent with the First Amendment rights of students.

The Supreme Court had clarified a student's right to read a book in the school library. Surely, Edwards argued, this right would extend to the school newspaper. She asked, what could distinguish the two? A student could choose to read the school newspaper, just as a student could choose to read a particular book located on a shelf in a school library. If a student was unhappy with the content of either the book or the paper, the student could choose not to read it. It was a choice that each student should have the freedom to make.

Edwards claimed that Reynolds censored the material because he did not agree with the message. In her argument, Edwards said that Reynolds's concern with the article on pregnancy was not that the *material* was inappropriate, but that the *message* was inappropriate. She said that previous articles published in *Spectrum* had discussed teen pregnancy, but, she argued, this article was different. It contained interviews with pregnant students who seemed optimistic about their futures. Previous articles published on the topic in *Spectrum* carried a more negative tone regarding the futures of the mothers. The school district, she argued, had no objection to the topic. That was evidenced by the fact that the prior teen pregnancy articles were not censored. However, Edwards said, the school board did not approve of the message of this particular article. The school district was concerned that younger students would read these articles and see that some pregnant high school students were planning bright futures for themselves and their children. Would this give the students the impression that getting pregnant in high school was not always a bad thing? Edwards argued that addressing the issue of teen pregnancy in *Spectrum* would help other students. It would draw attention to the issue and provide real-life accounts of pregnant students who were adjusting to their new lives.

Edwards also took issue with the fact that Reynolds had not given the students an opportunity to make changes to the articles. He made the decision to censor the paper without any input from the students and without even offering a platform for discussion. He decided almost immediately after reading the articles to delete the entire two-page spread of the May 13 edition. Edwards argued that Reynolds could have chosen other, less dramatic, courses of action. His actions, given the circumstances, were unreasonable. She claimed there was time to make changes to the articles, time to discuss alterations, and time to get consent from the divorced parents and fathers mentioned in the articles. Edwards said that

Reynolds had made no attempt to compromise with the staff. He exhibited complete and total control over the May 13 edition of the newspaper. Edwards claimed this control went beyond control over curriculum alone, as the school board had argued.

Control Over Curriculum or Ideas?

The school board had argued on numerous occasions that they were trying to maintain control over the curriculum of the school. It claimed that *Spectrum* was a laboratory assignment in the Journalism II class, and therefore it was part of the school curriculum. As part of the school curriculum, the school board could maintain control over the newspaper by having a faculty member advise the students. Final publication of each edition of *Spectrum* was also to be approved by the principal prior to printing.

Edwards focused one of her arguments on the school district's control over *Spectrum*. Obviously, the students needed guidance, she said, since they were only high school students and were working on their first newspaper. Surely they would need instruction, but where was the line between guidance and control over expression? Edwards argued that the school district knew of no line. The school district, Edwards claimed, misinterpreted its role with regard to *Spectrum*. It had taken its right to advise the students to a new level—a level that was unconstitutional.

National Support for the Students

Just as interested third parties submitted briefs in support of the school district, numerous organizations submitted *amicus curiae* briefs to the Supreme Court asking the Court to affirm the decision of the Court of Appeals. The ACLU, American Society of Newspaper Editors, People for the American Way, National Organization for Women Legal Defense and Education Fund, Planned Parenthood Federation of America, and Student Press Law Center all submitted briefs on behalf of the students. The groups collectively argued in favor of students' rights to free speech in their school newspaper.

Each side had submitted its briefs. The Court now had the opportunity to study the facts of the case and examine the legal arguments presented in the numerous briefs submitted to the Court. The justices would then ask Leslie Edwards numerous questions regarding the purpose of *Spectrum* and the authority of the *Spectrum* advisor. She argued that the censorship of *Spectrum* occurred simply because the school district did not approve of the content in the articles and the views expressed.

chapter 5

The Evolution of the Rights of Children

Currently, the rights of children receive some protections under United States law, though there is not nearly as much protection as adults receive. However, until the twentieth century, many children in the United States worked because they needed to help support their families. It was not seen as unusual to have young boys working on farms, in factories, or in the family trade. Young girls often worked within the home by helping their mothers with the housework, cooking, cleaning, and taking care of siblings. There was a time when children were preferred by company owners because they worked for less than adults and were easier to control.[1] In some communities, as soon as children were physically able to work, they were given a job. The majority of children were not educated. Often only the wealthy enjoyed that privilege. If a child did receive an education, it may not have extended beyond the eighth grade.

Children who were lucky enough to get an education had few rights within the school setting. School officials had nearly full control over the students and children were taught to obey. They were not to act disrespectfully toward a teacher or school official. During class hours, school officials took the place of the parents. If a student did act out, the teacher often punished the student with a spanking. Most parents did not complain or even take issue with the punishment; in fact, they often approved. School officials were merely reinforcing the discipline the children were receiving at home. Society and the law held that discipline could be administered any way a parent saw fit. Parents could also force their children to work very long hours. This child was their child, many parents thought, and they could do what they wanted with their own children.

This situation was about to change. Children were about to be seen as individuals, as people in need of protection. Society's view on children and their rights would soon be evolving. Would the lawmakers follow suit?

The Rights of Children in School

In the early twentieth century, children's rights—especially their right to safety—were getting more attention. Laws protecting children were being passed. There were now limits on the type of work children could do. Parents no longer were seen as having total control over their children. Parents suspected of neglect or abuse could receive punishment. Children were finally getting a voice.

The first case to go before the Supreme Court involving a child's rights in school was the case of *Meyer* v. *Nebraska.* In *Meyer,* a parochial school teacher in Hamilton County, Nebraska, Robert Meyer, was found guilty of violating a 1919 law. The law stated that in all public and private schools only English could be taught to children until they passed the eighth grade. Under this law, Meyer had been convicted for teaching German to Raymond Parpart, a ten-year-old student in a Lutheran school. The Nebraska Supreme Court upheld the conviction. Other states at that time had similar laws on the books. On June 4, 1923, the Supreme Court found the Nebraska law to be unconstitutional. The Court held that the law violated the liberty protected by the Due Process Clause of the Fourteenth Amendment. When a state regulates liberty, the Court held, it must have a good reason for doing

Until the last century, children were considered the property of their parents and could be put to work. This twelve-year-old girl worked long hours in a Vermont cotton mill for little pay.

so. This law, the Court held, seemed to have no reasonable purpose. According to the Court:

> As the statute undertakes to interfere only with teaching which involves a modern language, leaving complete freedom as to other matters, there seems no adequate foundation for the suggestion that the purpose was to protect the child's health by limiting his mental activities. It is well known that proficiency in a foreign language seldom comes to one not instructed at an early age, and experience shows that this is not injurious to the health, morals, or understanding of the ordinary child.[2]

This case gave rights to parents to make decisions about their children's education and as a result, broadened the rights of children. The best interest of children was getting recognition.

Focus on Freedom

Freedom is intangible: You can't touch it, feel it, or see it. People can go through their entire lives without ever acknowledging the freedoms they have enjoyed. But if a freedom is taken away from a person, it is a whole different story. Cathy, Leslie, and Leanne had enjoyed a certain amount of freedom in connection with their work with *Spectrum.* They understood that Robert Stergos had reserved the right to make corrections and offer guidance before Howard Emerson took over. But it was not until their work was completely cut out of the newspaper that they truly felt violated and realized the value of the freedom of speech.[3] Their freedom had been infringed. This did not sit well with them. So they did what many students did during that period of time—they fought for their rights.

During the 1960s, freedom became a hot topic. Protests were taking place all over the country. Various people were fighting for various causes. Minorities were fighting back against years of discrimination. Teenagers were fighting back against years of strict discipline. The word was getting out. If someone did not agree with something, they said it. Each person had a constitutional right to expression. Opposition had developed to the Vietnam War. Many Americans did not agree with the tactics being used in the war, the financial cost, or the loss of life. People were protesting the draft. It was a time when people stood together to challenge the government. Twenty years later, Leanne, Cathy, and Leslie were standing together to forge ahead with their fight.

chapter 6

Legal Precedent

Beginning in the 1960s, more attention was being given to personal freedoms, including the freedom of children at home and at school. One case that grabbed headlines was *Tinker* v. *Des Moines Independent School District.* This was the case that the Court of Appeals had relied on in examining the facts in *Hazelwood.*

The *Tinker* case involved three students: John F. Tinker, who was fifteen; his sister Mary Beth, who was thirteen; and Christopher Eckhardt, who was sixteen. In December 1965, a meeting was held at the home of Christopher Eckhardt. The group attending the meeting, both adults and children, decided to publicly display their objection to the U.S. involvement in the Vietnam War. They would wear black armbands during the holiday season to show their support for a truce. They would also fast on December 16 and New Year's Eve.[1]

Mary Beth was in junior high school at the time, while Christopher and John were in high school. The principals of their schools had become aware of their plan. On December 14, the schools formed a policy to deal with this issue. They would ask any students wearing armbands to remove them. If they refused, they would be suspended until they returned to school without the armband.

On December 16th, Mary Beth and Christopher wore black armbands to their respective schools. John wore his on December 17. Each of the students were sent home and suspended until they came back without their armbands. They did not return to school until after the New Year, when their protest was over.

Through their parents, the students filed a lawsuit claiming that their First Amendment rights had been violated. School officials claimed that they had prohibited the armbands so they could maintain order in the school. The school believed that the students' expression of their disapproval of United States involvement in Vietnam could create a disturbance because support on each side of the Vietnam debate was strong at that time. The Supreme Court, however, found no evidence to indicate this. They agreed that the students were passively expressing their feelings about the war by wearing a piece of black cloth, not more than two inches wide, on their arms. This expression was protected speech, the Court ruled in its 1969 decision. The Court stated that this expression by the students was similar to "pure speech." Pure speech consists of words, either verbal or written, that are generally noncommercial and not mixed with conduct. Pure speech is protected under the First Amendment.

The Court reiterated its decision from the *Meyer* v. *Nebraska* case, where it held:

> First Amendment rights, applied in light of the special characteristics of the school environment, are available to teachers and students. It can hardly be argued that either students or teachers shed their constitutional rights to freedom of speech or expression at the schoolhouse gate.[2]

Just as it was unconstitutional to prohibit the teaching of a foreign language to children below the eighth grade, it was unconstitutional to prohibit students from wearing armbands in protest of the conflict in Vietnam because the school could not demonstrate in any way that a disturbance was likely to arise as a result of the students' expression. The Court did acknowledge the fact that officials do need to maintain order in their schools, but it said that they did not need to do it by infringing on the First Amendment rights of students. The Court quoted language from an earlier

Supreme Court case, *West Virginia State Board of Education* v. *Barnette,* where it ruled that a student need not be forced to salute the American flag in the classroom:

> The Fourteenth Amendment, as now applied to the States, protects the citizen against the State itself and all of its creatures—Boards of Education not excepted. These have, of course, important, delicate, and highly discretionary functions, but none that they may not perform within the limits of the Bill of Rights. That they are educating the young for citizenship is reason for scrupulous protection of Constitutional freedoms of the individual, if we are not to strangle the free mind at its source and teach youth to discount important principles of our government as mere platitudes.[3]

The Court in *Tinker* stated that the school was merely fearful that a disturbance *could* result from the students' wearing the armbands in protest. Fear alone, the Court held, was not enough, and students need to feel as though they can voice their opinions even if they disagree with the majority. Clearly, the Court reasoned, the school district in *Tinker* did not oppose all political speech: Students in the school district had worn political campaign buttons, and other students even wore the Iron Cross, a symbol once associated with Nazism.[4] Therefore, when the school prohibited students from wearing black armbands, it was being inconsistent in its response to controversial expressions.

These are the Supreme Court justices who would decide the case of Hazelwood v. Kuhlmeier *in 1988 (with the exception of Justice Lewis Powell, standing second from the left, who had retired).*

The Court had ruled in favor of the students protesting the Vietnam conflict. In *Island Trees* v. *Pico,* it had ruled against the school district for pulling "controversial" books from the school library shelf. It seemed the Court was acknowledging the importance of student speech. The *Tinker* decision quoted language from an earlier case that expressed the importance of fostering student expression:

> The vigilant protection of constitutional freedoms
> is nowhere more vital than in the community of
> American schools. The classroom is peculiarly the
> "marketplace of ideas." The Nation's future
> depends upon leaders trained through wide
> exposure to that robust exchange of ideas which
> discovers truth "out of a multitude of tongues,"
> rather than through any kind of authoritative
> selection.[5]

With these cases, the Court had expanded the rights of children at school. Cathy, Leslie, and Leanne were hopeful that the Supreme Court would affirm the Court of Appeals decision. They thought that the Supreme Court might stay consistent in its view that student speech should be protected unless it could be shown that the speech would be disruptive.

Then the decision was announced in the case of *Bethel School District No. 403* v. *Fraser*. In this case, a student had been suspended for using offensive speech while nominating another student for student government. The Court ruled against Matthew Fraser by stating that his speech was not protected. The Court stated:

> We hold that petitioner School District acted
> entirely within its permissible authority in
> imposing sanctions upon Fraser in response to his
> offensively lewd and indecent speech. Unlike the
> sanctions imposed on the students wearing
> armbands in *Tinker*, the penalties imposed in this
> case were unrelated to any political viewpoint. . . .
> It was perfectly appropriate for the school to

disassociate itself to make the point to the pupils that vulgar speech and lewd conduct is wholly inconsistent with the "fundamental values" of public school education.[6]

It seemed as though student free speech rights had lost this round. Now schools would be permitted to discipline students for certain types of speech—speech the school considered "offensive."

How would this ruling effect the decision in the *Hazelwood* case? Would the Court follow its ruling in *Fraser,* or would it apply the standard set forth in *Tinker?* The long journey the students embarked on back in 1983 was about to come to an end. Would it be a happy ending for the students or the school district?

chapter 7

The Supreme Court Decides

On January 13, 1988, the Supreme Court justices issued the decision in the case of *Hazelwood* v. *Kuhlmeier*. It had been a long road. Finally, the students and the school district learned the answer: The Supreme Court reversed the decision of the Court of Appeals. The Court voted 5–3 in favor of the school district. Justice Byron White delivered the opinion of the Court. Along with Justices Sandra Day O'Connor, Antonin Scalia, John Paul Stevens, and Chief Justice William Rehnquist, he had found in favor of the school district. The written opinion set forth their decision and spelled out how they had reached it.

As the school district had hoped, the decision in *Fraser* had been a factor in the justices' ruling.

The Court recognized that students have First Amendment protections; however, those protections are not the same as those of adults.

In the written opinion, the Court first addressed its recent decision in *Fraser.* It had ruled that a public school need not tolerate speech that was inconsistent with its educational mission, even if that speech would be permitted outside the school environment. The Court quoted its opinion in *Fraser* and stated:

> "The determination of what manner of speech in the classroom or in school assembly is inappropriate properly rests with the school board," rather than with the federal courts. It is in this context that respondents' First Amendment claims must be considered.[1]

The Court stated that the circumstances surrounding the censorship needed to be examined. The Court held that the school board was at liberty to judge the appropriateness of material and make modifications based on that judgment.

Spectrum is Not a Public Forum

The Court stated that school facilities can be considered public forums only if the school, by its policy or practice, opened the facility to random use by the public or at least part of the public. This would include a student organization. They stated that a public forum is not created just by allowing limited discussion in the forum. In making its decision, the Court also pointed to the curriculum guide of the school, which had described *Spectrum* as the laboratory assignment for the Journalism II class. During the class, the students would apply the knowledge they gained in Journalism I. Journalism II was taught by a faculty member during class hours. Students received grades for their contribution to the class. During the 1982–1983 school year, Stergos maintained control over *Spectrum* before he left. The District Court's opinion outlined Stergos's responsibilities: He selected the editors, scheduled publication dates, decided on the number of pages for each issue, assigned story ideas to class members, advised students on the development of their stories, reviewed the use of quotations, edited stories, selected and edited the letters to the editor, and dealt with the printing company.[2] All of this, the Court found, was evidence that *Spectrum* was not intended to be a public forum.

The justices stated that the Court of Appeals was vague in its reasoning as to why *Spectrum* was a public forum. The Appeals Court had relied on the Statement of Policy published in *Spectrum,* which stated that the newspaper accepted all rights implied by the First Amendment. The Supreme Court, however, held that the Statement of Policy suggested that the school officials would not interfere with the students' exercising their First Amendment rights, but they found that it did not suggest that the school intended to create a public forum. This was because the school officials did not open *Spectrum* to random use by the general student population or even staff of *Spectrum.* It was intended, the Court found, to be a vehicle for students to learn about journalism and newspaper production in a supervised environment.

Tinker Does Not Apply

In its written opinion, the Court distinguished the situation in *Tinker* from that in the *Hazelwood* case. *Tinker* addressed the issue of student expression on school premises. This was not the question before them in this case, the justices stated. The question here was to what extent could the school officials exhibit authority over school-sponsored publications, theater productions, and other expressive activities that are connected with the school. These types of activities, the Court found, can be seen as part of the school, even though they are not conducted in a typical classroom setting. For instance, a school newspaper and a student theater production are both supervised by faculty members. Both are designed to teach the students techniques and skills and are therefore part of the curriculum. School officials, the Court found, can exercise control over these types of activities because they need to make sure that the students learn. They need to make sure that the material is

The Supreme Court upheld Mary Beth Tinker's right to wear a black armband to school to protest the Vietman War. However, it did not hold that the Tinker *ruling applied to the students in the* Hazelwood *case.*

suitable for all listeners or readers, and the school needs to set a high standard with regard to speech that is associated with the school. It was the Court's position that the school should have the ability to forbid inappropriate speech in any activity related to school curriculum. Although this is not the case in the world of journalists out in the field, it is the case in a school setting, according to the Court. School officials could exercise control over the style and content of *Spectrum* as long as the censorship is reasonably related to academic concerns.

Principal Reynolds Acted Reasonably

The Court found that Reynolds's actions were reasonable given the circumstances, and they agreed with the principal's actions on May 10, 1983. First, the decision noted that his privacy concerns were valid: The articles were not sensitive to the privacy interests of the parents in the divorce article and the fathers in the teen pregnancy article. They agreed that personal information was being disseminated, and that the people mentioned had not been afforded the opportunity to respond. This did not seem to create a balanced story, which should be the goal of all journalists.

The Court also affirmed Reynolds's concern that the content in the articles could be inappropriate for some of the younger students at Hazelwood East. In addition, the Court found that Reynolds was justified in being apprehensive because the paper could make its way to a student's home, where younger siblings could read it.

The Court also found Reynolds's belief that he had to act quickly to be legitimate. Given the circumstances, they agreed that Reynolds reasonably believed he had minutes to decide whether the two-page spread would be deleted, or if there would be no publication at all.

Ultimately, the justices disagreed with the Court of Appeals and found Reynolds's beliefs to be reasonable given his conversation with Emerson on May 10. The Court stated:

> Reynolds could reasonably have concluded that the students who had written and edited these articles had not sufficiently mastered those portions of the Journalism II curriculum that pertained to the treatment of controversial issues and personal attacks, the need to protect the privacy of individuals whose most intimate concerns are to be revealed in the newspaper, and "the legal, moral, and ethical restrictions imposed upon journalists within [a] school community" that includes adolescent subjects and readers.[3]

The Dissenting Opinion

Justices who do not agree with the majority have the opportunity to write a dissenting opinion that states the reasons they disagree with the majority view. In the *Hazelwood* case, Justice William Brennan delivered the dissenting opinion, joined by Justices Harry Blackmun and Thurgood Marshall. These three justices viewed *Spectrum* as a public forum established to give the students an opportunity to express their views. Their opinion referred to the policy statement stating that under *Tinker, Spectrum* enjoyed the freedoms of the First Amendment. According to the dissenting justices, the policy statement did not need to directly state that First Amendment protection was extended to the school newspaper. They felt the purpose of *Spectrum* was clear: It was a forum for student expression and the censorship was a breach of the school's promise to the students. As a result of this decision, the dissent stated, the students no longer would enjoy a forum for expression.

The dissent acknowledged this country's history of allowing school boards to control the daily operations of a school; however, this control was not absolute. The Court had intervened in the past, where necessary, to protect the rights of students. The Court had even applied the ruling in *Tinker* to some of those cases. The dissenting judges felt that it did not make sense for *Tinker* to apply only to certain categories of speech. How could it be unconstitutional to shield students from books that contained material

'Beat It, Kids — This Show Is For Adults Only'

Many newspapers criticized the Supreme Court's decision in the Hazelwood case. This editorial cartoon appeared in the St. Louis Post-Dispatch.

the school board did not approve of but acceptable to shield students from a newspaper that contained controversial material? The dissent argued that Reynolds deleted the material not because it would interfere with academics, but because the school board would disagree with the message of the articles.

The dissenting justices felt that the school officials had deleted material based on "inappropriate" content, and that they had done so in a brutal fashion.[4] They believed Reynolds made no effort to consult with the students about his concerns, and made no attempt to find a less intrusive way to remedy the problem he saw. This was an abuse of his authority and a violation of the students' rights and should not be condoned, the dissenting justices argued. The dissent finished with the following:

> Instead of teaching children to respect the diversity of ideas that is fundamental to the American system, and that our Constitution is a living reality, not parchment preserved under glass, the Court today teaches youth to discount important principles of our government as mere platitudes. The young men and women of Hazelwood East expected a civics lesson, but not the one the Court teaches them today.[5]

The decision was made. The students had lost. The rights of students throughout the country were going to be affected. Was this a decision a step backward? Baine did not think so. He stated:

> Again, this is an issue of the control of curriculum. I think that the *Tinker* case had been abused. The original basis for *Tinker* was good but some lower courts had expanded *Tinker* to the point where school officials would have had to permit the printing of anything students wrote.[6]

chapter 8

The Aftermath

The Supreme Court had decided in favor of the school district. Would balanced newspaper writing cease to exist because of the fear of censorship? There is a phenomenon called the chilling effect, a human instinct that can kick in when fear is present. For instance, if people are afraid they will be censored, they may censor themselves for fear of repercussions. Would the decision in *Hazelwood* have a chilling effect on student publications? The Student Press Law Center reported that from 1988 to 1989, after the *Hazelwood* decision, it had received 12 percent more calls. These calls were from students who felt they were being censored. There were also calls from advisors and teachers who felt their employment would be jeopardized if they did not censor certain materials.[1] From 1989 to early 1990, calls increased 170 percent.[2] Attention on censorship in schools was on the rise.

After the Decision

The decision in *Hazelwood* significantly affected another lawsuit over the issue of editorial control by school officials over high school publications. It was the case of *Planned Parenthood of Southern Nevada* v. *Clark County School District.* Planned Parenthood is a family planning program that provides clinical, educational, and counseling services to people for reproductive health. Planned Parenthood had submitted advertisements for publication in the high school newspaper, year-books, and athletic programs within the district. The advertisement read:

> PLANNED PARENTHOOD
> OF SOUTHERN NEVADA, INC.
> 601 South Thirteenth Street
> Las Vegas, Nevada 89101
> Routine Gynecological Exams
> Birth Control Methods
> Pregnancy Testing & Verification
> Pregnancy Counseling & Referral

The school district refused to allow the ads to run because the principal felt that the material discussing birth control and pregnancy was not appropriate for advertisements in the school publications.

Planned Parenthood filed a lawsuit in district court claiming that its First Amendment rights were violated when it was refused the right to advertise in the school publications. The district court found in favor of Planned Parenthood. This, however, was before the decision in *Hazelwood.* After the Supreme Court decided *Hazelwood,* the district court reconsidered its decision and found in favor of Clark County School District. Planned Parenthood appealed the decision, and the appeals court found that the censorship was not a violation of Planned Parenthood's First Amendment rights. The appeals court found that although the case was similar to *Hazelwood,* it was not exactly the same issue. Here, the speech restricted was coming from a third party—an independent organization not associated with the school in any way. The free speech of students was not at issue.

Hazelwood had caused a court to change its ruling. The repercussions of the *Hazelwood* decision had begun. The decision in *Planned Parenthood of Southern Nevada* v. *Clark County School District* stated:

> *Hazelwood* instructs that we are to invest high school educators with greater control over expressive activities that bear the school's imprimatur [approval] than other forms of speech or use of government facilities. Thus, in striking a balance between the schools' interests and Planned Parenthood's, we must assume that

school-sponsored publications are nonpublic and that unless the school's affirmatively intend to open a forum for indiscriminate use, restrictions reasonably related to the school's mission that are imposed on the content of school-sponsored publications do not violate the first amendment.[3]

Another case that examined the *Hazelwood* decision took place in Wooster, Ohio. In 2002, school officials at Wooster High School confiscated the student newspaper, *The Blade,* after it had run a story that discussed the school's policy regarding underage drinking. The school took issue with the story because the story quoted a student who admitted to drinking off campus. The school felt the information in the newspaper was defamatory. Students working on *The Blade* filed a lawsuit and asked the judge to prevent the school from confiscating editions of *The Blade* in the future.

The judge, James S. Gwin of the Northern District of Ohio, District Court, denied that request but did devise a test for determining a public forum in school. Using factors from the *Hazelwood* case plus factors from a case heard by the Sixth Circuit Court, he set forth nine factors that must be analyzed in order to determine if a newspaper is a public forum:

◇ whether it is produced as part of the high school curriculum;

◇ whether students receive credit and grades for producing the newspaper;

◇ whether or not production of the newspaper is supervised by a faculty member;

◇ whether the newspaper was ever produced without being part of the curriculum;

◇ what degree of control the administration and faculty advisor exercise;

◇ the school board's applicable written policy statements;

◇ the school's policy regarding the newspaper;

◇ the school's practices regarding the newspaper; and finally

◇ the nature of the newspaper or article and compatibility with the expressive activity.[4]

The court had to analyze each factor to determine whether the policies and practices of the school were consistent with those of a public forum. When these nine factors were applied to the situation with *The Blade,* the judge found *The Blade* to be a limited public forum. This case was settled before it went to trial. However, this case and the *Planned Parenthood* case show the disparity among the lower courts in their interpretation of the ruling in *Hazelwood.*

Censorship and Technology

It was only a matter of time before censorship of the Internet would become a matter of concern. People were online, surfing the World Wide Web. They were e-mailing each other, sending instant

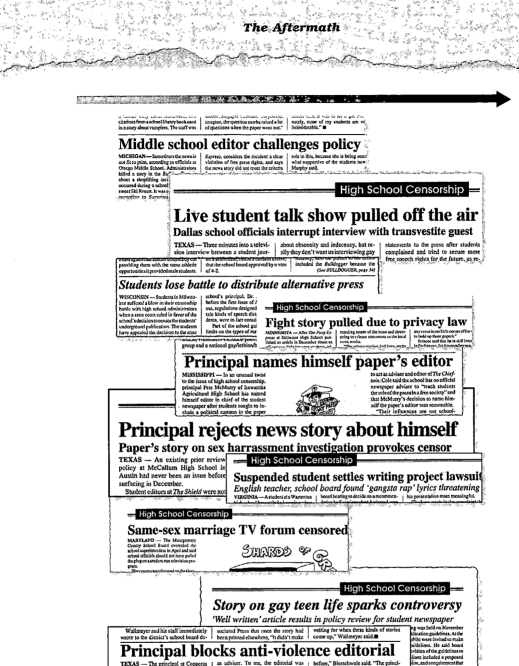

These headlines, compiled by the Student Press Law Center, show some of the impact the Hazelwood case has had on student journalism.

messages, text messaging, and communicating with people thousands of miles away in seconds. The world had changed since *Hazelwood* was decided. The way students could express themselves changed too. Soon censorship problems would plague the electronic world.

In 2003, the Supreme Court addressed one of the new issues in the case *United States* v. *American Library Association, Inc.* The question was whether public libraries could limit patrons' Internet access. Most public libraries receive federal money. Some of that money is used to provide Internet access to patrons.

Internet access in public libraries gained national attention when news surfaced that patrons of public libraries were using the Internet access to view pornography. Oftentimes, the images would be left on the screen for the next unsuspecting patron to view. This meant that children could view pornographic images or other obscene material while visiting their community library. As a response, Congress enacted the Children's Internet Protection Act (CIPA) in December of 2000, which forbids public libraries to receive federal money for Internet access unless they installed software to block obscene or pornographic material. The goal of this law was to prevent minors from accessing material harmful to them. Usually, the library would install a filter, which served as a barrier and prevented patrons from visiting certain Web sites. The problem was that the filter sometimes filtered educational or medical material based on its content. For instance, a search for information on breast cancer can cause certain Web sites to be blocked because of the word "breast." As a result, important information on health issues could not be accessed by any library patron, regardless of age. If information they wanted to access was blocked, adults could ask the librarian to unblock the Web site. The act was intended to shield children, not adults, from content that could be inappropriate for younger audiences.

A group of libraries, library patrons, Web site publishers, and others filed a suit stating that the filtering was infringing on patrons' constitutional rights. The district court agreed with them. It found the Act to be unconstitutional because it required libraries to use software that would restrict access based on content in a public forum.

In 2003, the case made its way to the Supreme Court, which ruled differently. The Court stated that even though the filter sometimes blocked material that was not considered pornographic, it did not violate the Constitution because the government has an interest in protecting minors from obscene material. The Court stated:

> A library's need to exercise judgment in making
> collection decisions depends on its traditional role
> in identifying suitable and worthwhile material;
> it is no less entitled to play that role when it

> collects material from the Internet than when it collects material from any other source. Most libraries already exclude pornography from their print collections because they deem it inappropriate for inclusion. We do not subject these decisions to heightened scrutiny; it would make little sense to treat libraries' judgments to block online pornography any differently, when these judgments are made for just the same reason.[5]

Clearly, censorship issues were evolving with the times. The Supreme Court upheld a decision that allowed public libraries to block information from its patrons. The decision in *Hazelwood* gave school officials broad authority to censor speech and expression if it conflicted with educational goals. A school no longer had to show that there was a compelling reason for censorship, just a legitimate reason that was related to education. Opponents feared schools would be given almost complete control over student speech. Either way, *Hazelwood* was a monumental case in history. The case brought by three students from Missouri had made the history books. Whether the Court was right or wrong is for each person to decide, but one thing is for sure: Debate about this issue will live on.

chapter 9

Moot Court: Your Turn to Debate

Now it's your turn to debate the issues. In this chapter, you will learn how to participate in a moot court exercise.[1] You will learn how to research issues, write briefs, and even argue before the panel of judges. This exercise will help you get a feel for a courtroom and see just how a case is heard and decided.

A moot court is a dramatization of a case that has already received a ruling, either by an appeals court or the Supreme Court. The purpose of the appeal is to determine if the lower court erred in a way that was harmful to one of the parties named in the lawsuit. No witnesses will be called, because the facts are not in dispute. At this level, application of the law and procedural issues are disputed.

Try a moot court activity with your class or club. Members of the group will be assigned roles. Some students will act as judges. Others will be the attorneys, clerks, and members of the press, and one will even act as the bailiff.

Step 1: Assign Roles

The following roles will need to be assigned to different students:

◇ Judges. If the group is large enough, choose nine justices, just like the Supreme Court. If your group is too small for this, select three judges. You can have a moot court exercise with a three-judge panel, as many appellate courts conduct their sessions with a three-judge panel. Judges will hear oral arguments by both sides. They will ask the attorneys questions regarding their positions. After they hear the arguments, the judges will meet, discuss the case, and render a decision in the matter. The decision of the court will be based on the majority opinion of the judges. A majority opinion will be written and will become law. Judges can choose to write a concurring opinion, stating they agree with the majority and the reasons why. Judges can also choose to write a dissenting opinion, stating the reasons why they disagree with the majority. It is not uncommon for judges to agree with some findings by the majority and disagree with other findings of the majority.

◇ Two or more court clerks. Law clerks have a very important job in the court system. They review petitions for writ of certiorari, conduct research for the opinions of the judges, and they help the judges construct the questions to ask the attorneys. Being a law clerk for a United States Supreme Court justice is a much-coveted position. The Chief Justice can hire up to five law clerks, and the remaining eight justices can hire up to four law clerks each.

◇ A team of two or more attorneys for the appellant (the school district). They will try to persuade the court to find that the lower court ruled incorrectly.

◇ A team of two or more attorneys for the appellees (the students). The appellee is the party that wants the lower court decision to be upheld. Only one attorney for the appellants and one attorney for the appellees will be chosen to be the spokesperson. These attorneys will present the arguments to the judges. They must be persuasive because they must sway the opinions of the majority of the judges. Although the spokespeople will do most of the arguing for their side, other attorneys on their team are permitted to answer questions from the judges.

◇ Two or more reporters. When a case reaches the U.S. Supreme Court, it is newsworthy. Oftentimes, there are hundreds of news reporters covering the story. The reporters will interview the attorneys for each side

before and after the arguments. They will
then prepare their stories for the television
station, newspaper, or Internet sites they
represent.

◇ The bailiff. This person will call the Court to
order and keep track of the time for the oral
arguments.

Step 2: Prepare Your Case

You will need to perform three steps in order to be
prepared to argue in this moot court exercise.

Part 1: Gather Information

The case you will hear is *Hazelwood School
District* v. *Kuhlmeier* (1987). As you know, this
case involved three students of Hazelwood East
High School who were staff members of *Spectrum*,
the school newspaper. The May 13 edition was censored because certain faculty members of
Hazelwood East felt the content was inappropriate.
They also were concerned that some of the statements made in the articles could violate the
privacy rights of individuals mentioned. The students sued the school in federal court and lost
during the first trial. On appeal, the decision was
reversed. The Court of Appeals for the Eighth
Circuit held that the students' constitutional rights
were violated. The school district appealed that
decision and now the case is in front of your mock
Supreme Court.

Students in Maine participate in a mock trial. Taking part in judicial exercises is fun as well as being good for research, reasoning, and debating skills.

Everyone participating in the moot court activity should look at the *Hazelwood* case. Your public library may have Supreme Court cases. The *Hazelwood* case is at 484 U.S. 260. That is volume 484 of *United States Reports,* starting at page 260. You can find the case online too.[2] You may also wish to look at some of the related cases, such as *Tinker* and *Fraser*, to bolster your arguments.

Part 2: Write Your Briefs

Each party must write a legal brief setting forth the arguments of their client and the interpretation of the law relevant to the issues of the case. Attorneys for each side should discuss which arguments are the strongest and focus on those arguments. It is also helpful to anticipate arguments the opposing side will make and address them in your brief. Your argument must persuade the court to find in your client's favor. You must demonstrate to the judges why your client's position is the correct position.

The following are some arguments to get you started. Use these arguments as a springboard for discussion among the attorneys on your team.

◇ Hazelwood School District (appellant team): The school district did not violate the constitutional rights of the students because *Spectrum* was not a forum for the general public. It was never intended to be used as such. Therefore, the *Spectrum* staff was not entitled to First Amendment protection. *Spectrum* was a laboratory assignment for the Journalism II class. It was subject to control by the advisor. The staff members of *Spectrum* knew that approval was necessary for each edition of the newspaper. They were well aware that they did not have free rein to publish whatever they wanted. Although adults working for a newspaper enjoy First Amendment protection, students attending a public school do not enjoy those same protections.

◇ Staff members of *Spectrum* (appellee team): Hazelwood East High School intended *Spectrum* to be a limited public forum because the school offered access to people other than students of Hazelwood East. The policy statement printed in *Spectrum* during the beginning of each school year indicated that the students were free to publish what they considered newsworthy and that those items did not necessarily represent the ideas of the school or its teachers. *Spectrum* was a newspaper written, designed, and distributed by the students for the purposes of disseminating their viewpoints. The students should enjoy the same First Amendment protections as journalists in the field.

When a petitioner is granted certiorari by the Supreme Court, the attorneys on each side look to the court rules to see exactly what their brief must include. For this moot court exercise, use the following rules for your brief:

1. Your brief must contain a cover page. It must contain the case name, *Hazelwood School District* v. *Kuhlmeier.* List the attorneys for your team and whether you represent the appellee or appellant.

2. You must include the following in the body of your brief:

    A. Statement of the issues for review: What question is the court answering?

    B. Statement of the case: What is the case about? What did the trial court rule? What was the decision of the appeals court?

    C. Statement of facts: Describe the relevant facts of your case. Be concise.

    D. Summary of the argument: Summarize your argument in 150 words or less.

    E. Argument: Explain legal arguments that support your position. You must reference case law or statutory law that supports your position. You may want to include subheadings for your points so they are clearly conveyed to the reader.

    F. Conclusion: Ask the judges to find in your client's favor.

3. Unlike real legal briefs, which can be quite lengthy, this brief should be no more than five pages long, double spaced, approximately 1,250 words.

4. The teams of attorneys need to agree on a date to exchange information. On that date,

each side will give the other side a copy of their brief. Each judge will receive a copy as well. In your moot court exercise, it may be helpful for each student and your teacher to have a copy so they can follow the arguments of each side. In everyday practice, attorneys have the opportunity after they read the other teams' brief, to file a reply brief, addressing the issues that were raised in their opponents' brief. This will not be necessary in your moot court exercise. Be prepared to rebut the arguments raised in the opponents' brief. Be familiar with your opponents' arguments set forth in the brief.

Part 3: Prepare for Oral Arguments

The judges should be very familiar with the facts of the case before the oral arguments begin. That way, they can ask the attorneys questions about the case and the issues of the law. The judges should have at least a few questions planned before the arguments begin. It is likely that the judges will think of questions as they hear the arguments.

Each side will have fifteen minutes to make their arguments. It is crucial that you practice your arguments beforehand so you can be certain that you are hitting the most important points of your case within the time allotment. Fifteen minutes is not a long time, and you want to maximize it.

Do not interrupt a judge when he or she is asking a question. It is considered disrespectful to the court. Be prepared to answer questions from the judges. Practice with your teammates possible questions and responses. This will help you get more comfortable with the material.

Step 3: Hold the Oral Argument

Part 1: Assemble the Participants

◇ The judges will sit as a panel at the front of the room. This is called the bench. A podium or lectern will be positioned in front of the panel, facing the judges.

◇ The team of attorneys for the school district will sit on one side of the room, facing the judges.

◇ The team for Cathy, Leslie, and Leanne will sit on the other side of the room.

◇ The news reporters will sit at the back of the room and take notes.

◇ The bailiff will stand toward the front of the room, off to the side.

Part 2: Present the Case

◇ As the judges enter the room, the Bailiff will call the court to order: "Oyez (oy-yay)! Oyez! Oyez! The _____Court of the United States is now in session with the Honorable Chief Justice _____ presiding. All will stand and remain standing until the judges are seated and the Chief Justice has asked all present to be seated."

◇ The Chief Justice will then ask everyone to be seated. He or she will then call the case and ask whether the parties are ready to begin their oral arguments. The spokespersons for the attorneys will then both answer "Yes" if they are ready.

◇ The appellant's team will begin first. The spokesperson for the team of attorneys for the school district will begin by stating, "May it please the Court." The argument begins. Should a judge ask a question, the attorney must stop and answer the question before moving on to another point in his or her argument. The appellant's team has the right to allot five minutes of its time to rebut the arguments from the opposing side. If the attorneys for the appellant wish to do so, they should notify the judges before being seated.

◇ The appellee's team then argues its position for fifteen minutes by discussing the most important points in their case and trying to persuade the judges to agree with them.

◇ After the arguments are completed, the bailiff asks everyone in the courtroom to rise as the judges leave and go back to their chambers. There the judges will discuss the case and come to a decision. It is best to allot a specific amount of time for the judges to deliberate. The attorneys are free to answer questions from the public at this point. The reporters should take this opportunity to interview the attorneys. They should ask the attorneys how they think their arguments fared, what they thought of the questions asked, and how they think the judges might decide.

◇ After the deliberation time ends, the judges will return to the room, where the Chief Justice will announce the decision of the Court.

Step 4: Publish and Report the Decision

The final step in this moot court exercise is the written opinion. The Court will issue the majority opinion, along with any dissenting opinions and any individual concurring opinions. If one of the judges agreed with the majority on most points but disagreed on a specific point, that judge can write a dissent, which is his or her statement of why he or she disagreed with the majority on that issue. The same can be said if a judge disagreed with the majority on the ruling but agreed on a specific point. That judge can write a concurring opinion, which sets forth the reasons he or she agreed with the majority on that one specific point.

At this point, the news reporters distribute their articles on the debate to the students and teacher of the class.

Questions for Discussion

1. Do you think the material that the school censored was inappropriate considering the age of some of the younger students at Hazelwood? Why or why not?

2. Do you think the departure of Robert Stergos had anything to do with the breakdown in communication between the students and the school district? Do you think the students would have filed a lawsuit if Stergos had been communicating with Reynolds on May 10?

3. The Supreme Court has clearly indicated that minors do not have the same rights as adults. Do you agree? Why or why not?

4. Do you think the decision in Hazelwood resulted in a chilling effect in student publications? Do students censor themselves as a result of the decision?

5. The Supreme Court held that a school-sponsored newspaper is not a public forum for expression. Do you agree?

6. Hazelwood Principal Ronald Eugene Reynolds testified that he believed he had to act immediately when he received the proofs of the

May 13 edition of *Spectrum* containing the controversial articles. Do you think that this belief was reasonable?

7. The students testified that they believed they could publish almost anything in *Spectrum*. The court was not swayed by their testimony. Are you?

Chapter 1. Censorship 101

1. Hazelwood Joint Appendix, Defendant's Exhibit B, p. 8.

2. *Kuhlmeier* v. *Hazelwood School District*, 607 F. Supp. 1450, 1452 (1985).

3. *Kuhlmeier* v. *Hazelwood School District*, 607 F. Supp. 1450, 1453 (1985).

4. Ibid.

5. *Kuhlmeier* v. *Hazelwood School District*, 607 F. Supp. 1450, 1458 (1985).

6. "State of Missouri Families: Trend in the Number of Divorces," *Missouri Families: Learning Opportunities for Families*, December 3, 2002, <http://missourifamilies.org/report/trends/divorce.htm> (August 10, 2005).

7. *Kuhlmeier* v. *Hazelwood School District*, 795 F 2d 1368, 1376 (1986).

8. *Kuhlmeier* v. *Hazelwood School District*, 607 F. Supp. 1450, 1457 (1985).

9. Ibid.

10. *Kuhlmeier* v. *Hazelwood School District*, 607 F. Supp. 1450, 1456 (1985).

Chapter 2. The Legal Journey Begins

1. *Kuhlmeier* v. *Hazelwood School District*, 607 F. Supp. 1450, (1985).

2. *Kuhlmeier* v. *Hazelwood School District*, 795 F. 2d 1368, 1372 (1986).

3. *Kuhlmeier* v. *Hazelwood School District*, 607 F. Supp. 1450, 1456 (1985).

4. *Kuhlmeier* v. *Hazelwood School District*, 607 F. Supp. 1450, 1454 (1985).

5. *Kuhlmeier* v. *Hazelwood School District*, 607 F. Supp. 1450, 1454–1455 (1985).

6. *Tinker v. Des Moines Independent Community School District,* 393 U.S. 503, 512 (1969).

7. Ibid.

Chapter 3. The Case for the School District

1. *"Hazelwood School District v. Kuhlmeier* (Oral Argument)," *Oyez: U. S. Supreme Court Multimedia,* n.d., <http://www.oyez.org/oyez/resource/case/158/audioresources > (August 10, 2005).

Chapter 4. The Case for the Students

1. *"Hazelwood School District v. Kuhlmeier* (Oral Argument)," *Oyez: U. S. Supreme Court Multimedia,* n.d., <http://www.oyez.org/oyez/resource/case/158/audioresources > (August 10, 2005).

2. Ibid.

3. Ibid.

4. *Board of Education, Island Trees Union Free School District No. 26 v. Pico,* 457 U.S. 853, 856–857 (1982).

Chapter 5. The Evolution of the Rights of Children

1. "Child Labor in U.S. History," *Child Labor Public Education Project,* n.d., <http://www.continuetolearn. uiowa.edu/laborctr/child_labor/about/us_history.html> (November 22, 2005).

2. *Meyer v. Nebraska,* 262 U.S. 390, 403 (1923).

3. *Kuhlmeier v. Hazelwood School District,* 607 F. Supp. 1450, 1459 (1985).

Chapter 6. Legal Precedent

1. *Tinker v. Des Moines Independent Community School District,* 393 U.S. 503, 504 (1969).

2. *Tinker v. Des Moines Independent Community School District,* 393 U.S. 503, 506 (1969).

3. *West Virginia State Board of Education v. Barnette,* 319 U.S. 624, 637 (1943).

4. *Tinker v. Des Moines Independent Community School District,* 393 U.S. 503, 507 (1969).

5. *Tinker v. Des Moines Independent Community School District,* 393 U.S. 503, 512 (1969), quoting *Keyishan* v. *Board of Regents of University of State of N.Y.,* U.S. 589, 603 (1967).

6. *Bethel School District No. 403 v. Fraser,* 478 U.S. 675, 685–686 (1986).

Chapter 7. The Supreme Court Decides

1. *Hazelwood School District v. Kuhlmeier,* 484 U.S. 260, 267 (1988).

2. *Kuhlmeier v. Hazelwood School District,* 607 F. Supp. 1450, 1453 (1985).

3. *Hazelwood School District v. Kuhlmeier,* 484 U.S. 260, 276 (1988).

4. *Hazelwood School District v. Kuhlmeier,* 484 U.S. 260, 290 (1988).

5. *Hazelwood School District v. Kuhlmeier,* 484 U.S. 260, 277 (1988).

6. David Hudson, "Cathy Cowan reflects on her high school journalism fight in *Hazelwood* case," *Freedom Forum,* December 27, 2001, <http://www.freedomforum. org/templates/document.asp?documentID=15516> (November 22, 2005).

Chapter 8. The Aftermath

1. "The Hazelwood Decision and Student Press: A Complete Guide to the Supreme Court Decision," *Scholastic,* n.d.,<http://teacher.scholastic.com/researchtools/ articlearchives/civics/usgovt/judic/hazstupr.htm> (August 10, 2005).

2. Ibid.

3. *Planned Parenthood of Southern Nevada v. Clark County School District,* 941 U.S. F 2d 817, 819 (1991).

4. *Draudt v. Wooster City School District Board of*

Education, Case No. 5:03-CV-62 (N.D. Ohio February 14, 2003).

5. *United States* v. *American Library Association, Inc.,* 539 U.S. 194, 225 (2003).

Chapter 9. Moot Court: Your Turn to Debate

1. Adapted from Millie Aulbur, "Constitutional Issues and Teenagers," *The Missouri Bar,* n.d., <http://www.mobar.org/teach/clesson.htm> (December 10, 2004); Street Law, Inc., and The Supreme Court Historical Society, "Moot Court Activity," 2002, <http://www.landmarkcases.org> (December 10, 2004); with suggestions from Ron Fridell and Kathiann M. Kowalski.

2. See Legal Information Center, "Supreme Court Collection: *Hazelwood School District* v. *Kuhlmeier* (No. 86-836)," n.d, <http://straylight.law.cornell.edu/supct/search/display.html?terms=hazelwood&url=supct/html> (November 21, 2005); and "Landmark Supreme Court Cases: *Hazelwood* v. *Kuhlmeier* (1988)," n.d., <http://www.landmarkcases.org/hazelwood/home.html> (November 21, 2005).

Further Reading

Allport, Alan. *Freedom of Speech*. Philadelphia: Chelsea House Publishers, 2003.

Foerstel, Herbert N. *From Watergate to Monicagate: Ten Controversies in Modern Journalism and Media*. Westport, Conn.: Greenwood Press, 2001.

Friedman, Ian C. *Freedom of Speech and the Press*. New York: Facts on File, 2005.

Hebert, David L., editor. *Freedom of the Press*. San Diego: Greenhaven Press, 2005.

Hinchey, Patricia H. *Student Rights: A Reference Handbook*. Santa Barbara, Calif.: ABC-CLIO, 2001.

Irons, Peter, editor. *May It Please the Court: Courts, Kids, and the Constitution*. New York: New Press, 2000.

Isler, Claudia. *The Right to Free Speech*. New York: Rosen Publishing Group, 2001.

Jacobs, Thomas A. *Teens on Trial: Young People Who Challenged the Law—and Changed Your Life*. Minneapolis, Minn.: Free Spirit Publishing, 2000.

Internet Addresses

First Amendment Center

http://www.firstamendmentcenter.org/faclibrary/
case.aspx?id=1242

Landmark Supreme Court Cases

http://www.landmarkcases.org/hazelwood/
home.html

Student Press Law Center

http://www.splc.org/legalresearch.asp?id=4

Index

About the Author

Tracy A. Phillips is a consumer rights attorney, certified mediator, and editorial staff member of a legal journal. *Hazelwood v. Kuhlmeier and the School Newspaper Censorship Debate: Debating Supreme Court Decisions* is her first book for Enslow Publishers, Inc.